# Contents

# Your body

What is the colour of
your skin, eyes and hair?
Is your hair long or
short, straight or curly?
What shape are you?
Are you tall or short?

We are all
different.
No one looks
exactly like
you. This
makes you
special.

Keeping fit helps your
body to stay **healthy**.
You also need
plenty of rest,
and to eat three
meals a day.

Your body is made up of millions of tiny **cells**. They make up your **bones**, skin, **blood** and all the other parts of your body.

You will use your body all your life, so it is important to look after yourself.

It's important to get plenty of sleep, so that you have lots of energy in the morning.

# Keeping fit

When you **exercise**, you use many different parts of your body. Regular exercise keeps you fit and healthy.

Exercising makes your **heart** and **lungs** work hard, and this makes them strong.

head

neck

shoulder

elbow

chest

hand

finger

hip

leg

thigh

knee

ankle

foot

toe

If you are fit and healthy, you will have lots of energy for running and playing.

Which parts of your body do you use when you run? Do you use the same parts when you swim?

Swimming is a great way to exercise. It uses most of the **muscles** in your body.

7

# Exercise is fun!

Your body works better when it is used a lot. Think of the things you like to do. Running, playing football, skipping, cycling and roller skating all help to keep you fit.

Your body may become stiff if you do not use it.

Bending and stretching are other ways of exercising your body.

When you exercise, you breathe quickly. If you have been exercising hard, it may take a few minutes to get your breath back.

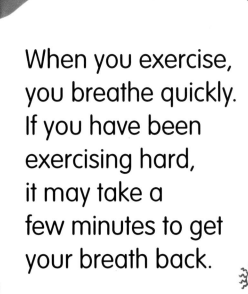

9

# What makes me move?

Muscles make you move. You use your muscles when you play games, run, swim, breathe, smile and talk. Your heart is a muscle, too. It beats without you thinking about it.

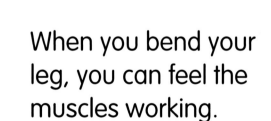

When you bend your leg, you can feel the muscles working.

Many muscles work in pairs. As you bend your arm, the biceps muscle pulls your arm up. The triceps muscle pulls in the other direction and straightens out your arm. Muscles are attached to your bones by bands called tendons.

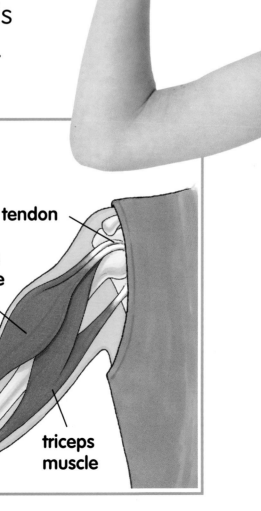

tendon

biceps muscle

bone

triceps muscle

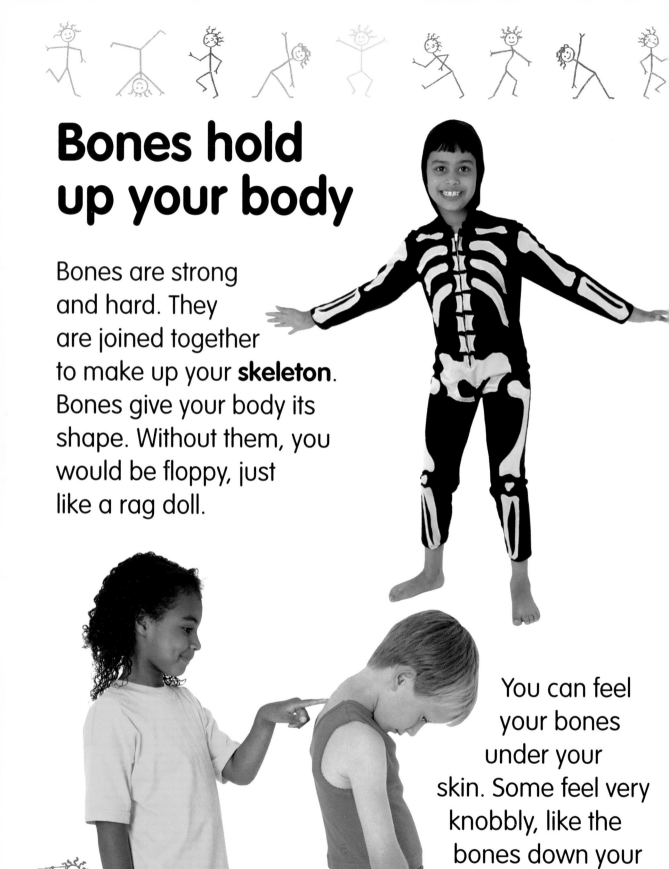

# Bones hold up your body

Bones are strong and hard. They are joined together to make up your **skeleton**. Bones give your body its shape. Without them, you would be floppy, just like a rag doll.

You can feel your bones under your skin. Some feel very knobbly, like the bones down your back (your spine).

You have 27 bones in each hand. The bones in your fingers feel smooth and straight.

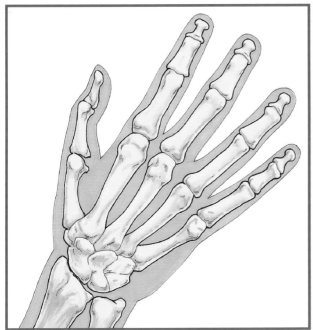

Bones protect the soft parts inside your body from injury. Your **skull** protects your brain and your **ribs** protect your heart and lungs.

13

# What are joints?

Bones are hard and do not bend. Your body can only bend at the joints. These are the places where two bones meet.

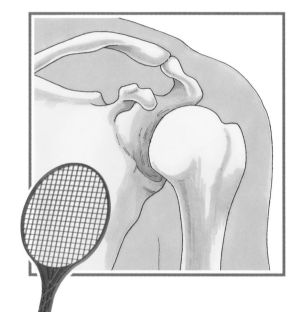

Your arm is attached to your shoulder by a **ball and socket joint**.

A ball and socket joint allows you to move your arm in almost any direction.

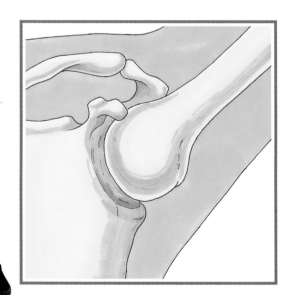

Try swinging your arms round and round and up and down.

Your hips have ball and socket joints, too

Your elbows and knees are **hinge joints**. They can only move backwards and forwards, like a door hinge.

You also have hinge joints in your fingers.

15

# Broken bones

Bones grow and change shape just like the rest of you. And when they break, they mend themselves.

A break in a bone is called a fracture. A **plaster cast** keeps the broken pieces of bone firmly together.

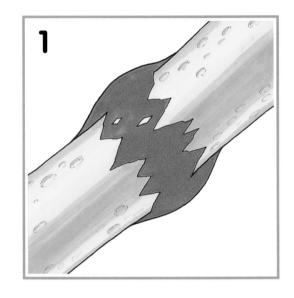

1

**1** When a bone breaks, blood around the break hardens and covers the broken ends.

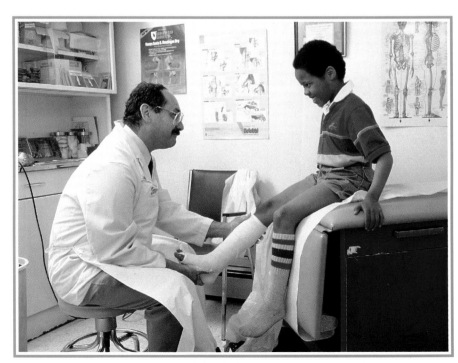

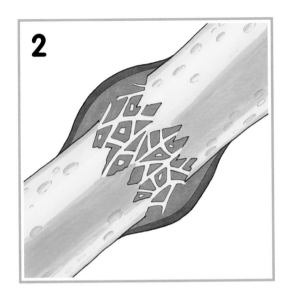

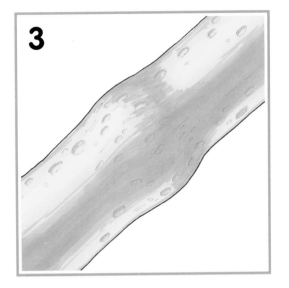

**2** New bone grows on each side of the break, and joins the broken bones together.

**3** After about 12 weeks, the break has **healed**, and the plaster cast can be taken off.

Bones are hard and strong, but they may break if you fall or have an accident.

# Skin deep

Skin is waterproof and very tough. It keeps harmful things, such as dust and **germs**, out of your body.

Your skin is soft, but stretchy. It allows you to move about.

Your skin never wears out! Old skin cells are replaced by new ones all the time.

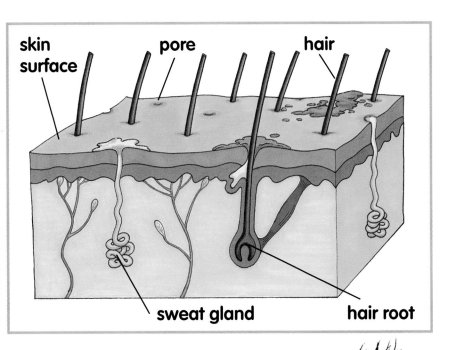

skin surface

pore

hair

sweat gland

hair root

This is a drawing of the surface of your skin. When you are cold, the hairs stand up straight.

Skin keeps you cool. When you run, your body becomes hot, and **sweat** oozes out of your skin through tiny holes called pores.

As the sweat trickles over your skin, your body cools down.

19

# Cuts and grazes

If you **graze** or cut yourself, blood trickles out of your skin. Soon the blood stops and dries to form a hard **scab**. The scab covers the wound and stops germs getting into your body.

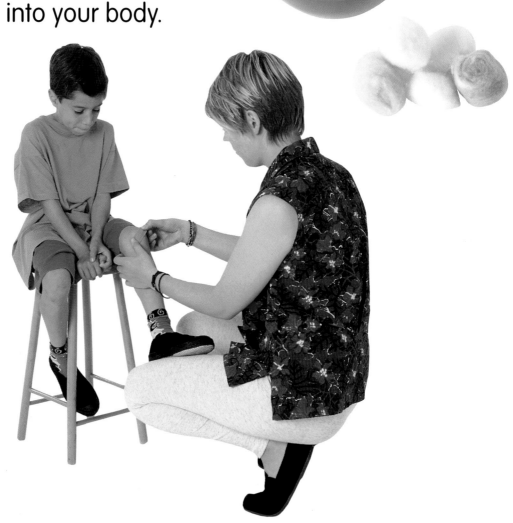

Wash the wound
with water to clean it.
A **bandage** or **plaster**
helps to keep out
the germs.

A scab forms to
protect the broken skin.

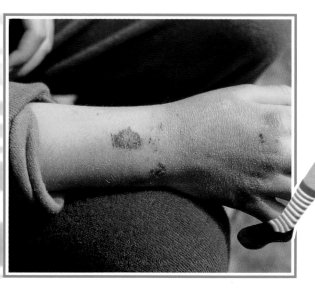

New skin cells grow
under the scab, and the
wound starts to heal.

Don't pick at the
scab! It will fall off
when the skin is
completely healed.

21

# Too much sun

Playing out in the sun is fun.
It makes you feel good.
But too much
sun can be
harmful.

If you are badly
**sunburnt**, your skin
turns red and sore.

Painful bubbles
of fluid, called
blisters, may form
on the burnt skin.

22

Doctors believe that too much sunlight causes a dangerous **disease** called skin cancer. This can be treated, but it is best to avoid too much sun.

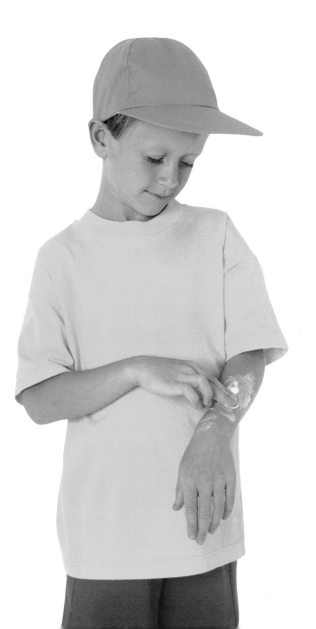

**Cover Up!**
Wear a hat and T-shirt. Use a special cream to protect your skin. Stay in the shade when the sun is at its strongest during the middle of the day.

23

# Feeling ill

Have you ever had a cough or cold? It is best to stay in bed when you are feeling ill.

If your illness does not go away, you should see a doctor. He or she will decide what treatment will make you better.

You may have to go to a hospital if your illness is serious. The doctors and nurses will look after you. If you need to stay in hospital, your mum or dad, or a grown-up friend, can usually stay with you.

# Protecting against disease

Is it true that coughs and sneezes spread diseases? Yes!

When you sneeze, air shoots out of your mouth and nose at about 160 km per hour – the speed of a hurricane. So do not cough or sneeze over other people!

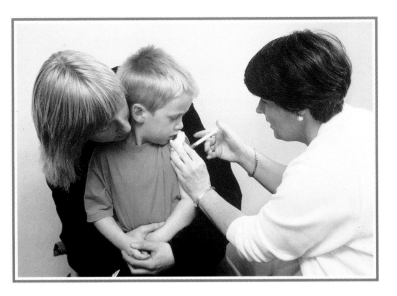

Doctors protect you against serious diseases by giving you an **injection** or some medicine to swallow.

Chickenpox and mumps are two diseases that most people get when they are young. Once you have had them, you are unlikely to get them again.

# Keeping clean

Keeping clean keeps your body healthy. It's important to wash every day, and to keep your hair clean.

Germs are all around you, even though you can't see them. Always wash your hands before eating, and after you have been to the toilet.

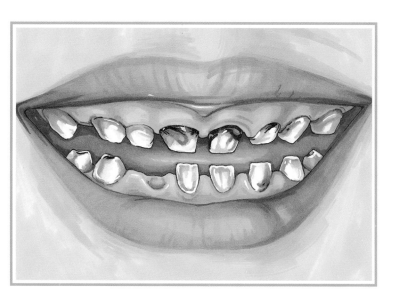

If you do not brush your teeth regularly your teeth may **decay**.

Every day your skin **sheds** millions of dead cells, and produces **oils** and sweat. If these stay on your skin for long, your body begins to smell nasty.

# Useful words

**Ball and socket joint**
A joint that can move in many different directions.

**Bandage**
A special covering for a wound.

**Blood**
The red liquid that is pumped around your body by your heart.

**Bones**
The strong and hard parts of your body.

**Cells**
Tiny parts that make up your body.

**Decay**
To go bad or to rot.

**Disease**
Illness or sickness.

**Exercise**
Using your body by running, swimming, cycling, and so on.

**Germs**
Living things that are too small to be seen with the naked eye. They can make you ill.

**Graze**
To scrape your skin against something hard.

**Healed**
Made healthy again.

**Healthy**
Strong and well.

**Heart**
The muscle that pumps blood around your body.

**Hinge joints**
Joints that move backwards and forwards.

**Injection**
A way of protecting you against illness.

**Lungs**
The spongy areas in your chest that you use when breathing.

**Muscles**
The soft, stretchy parts of your body that make you move.

**Oils**
Greasy liquids from the skin.

**Plaster**
A small covering for a cut or graze.

**Plaster cast**
A strong covering for a broken bone.

**Ribs**
The bones in your chest.

**Scab**
The hard crust that forms over a cut or graze.

**Shed**
To throw off.

**Skeleton**
The bones in your body.

**Skull**
The bony part of your head.

**Sunburnt**
To have burnt skin after being in the hot sun.

**Sweat**
Wetness from the skin.

# Index

# Why Do I Feel Hungry?

ms⁷/₉₉ ⁱons about

system

nwell

y

ski, Jr.

nt

AKE

First published in Great Britain by Moondrake
Halley Court, Jordan Hill, Oxford OX2 8EJ,
a division of Reed Educational & Professional Publishing Ltd

OXFORD  FLORENCE  PRAGUE  MADRID  ATHENS  MELBOURNE
AUCKLAND  KUALA LUMPUR  SINGAPORE  TOKYO  IBADAN
NAIROBI  KAMPALA  JOHANNESBURG  GABORONE
PORTSMOUTH NH (USA)  CHICAGO  MEXICO CITY  SAO PAULO

First published 1997

01 00 99 98
10 9 8 7 6 5 4 3 2 1

ISBN 0 431 06159 9
This title is also available in hardback (ISBN 0 431 06158 0)

**British Library Cataloguing in Publication Data**

Cromwell, Sharon
  Why do I feel hungry? – (Body wise)
  1. Human anatomy – Juvenile literature   2. Human physiology –
  Juvenile literature   3. Body, Human – Juvenile literature
  I. Title
  612

Printed in Hong Kong by Wing King Tong Co. Ltd.

Every effort has been made to contact the copyright holders of any material reproduced in this book.
Any omissions will be rectified in subsequent printings if notice is given to the publisher.